Happy Nola
Love Jmu

JM 2016

To
my city of New Orleans and my state Louisiana
for the many cultures and flavors without them
I wouldn't be me or have material for this book.

Follow Juju:
www.JujuTheGoodVoodoo.com
facebook.com/JujuTheGood
Twitter @JujuGoodVoodoo
Instagram @JujuTheGoodVoodoo
etsy.com/shop/JujuTheGoodVoodoo

Special Thanks to my Awesome contributors:
Diann Hirstius, Tayler Hirstius and Mary Wagner

writings and illustrations copyright © 2013 by Michelle Hirstius
All rights reserved. No part of this book may be reproduced, transmitted, or stored in an information retrieval system in any form or by any means, graphic, electronic, or mechanical, including photocopying, taping, and recording, without the prior written permission from the publisher.

Summary: Juju brings ABCs to life with New Orleans culture and facts.

Second Edition
ISBN-13: 978-0-9859202-2-7
ISBN-10: 098592022X

Illustrations done in crayon and ink by: Michelle Hirstius.

Fleur de Dat, LLC
P.O. Box 930
Mandeville, LA 70470-0930

www.fleurdedat.com

Juju's
NOLA ABCs and Fun Facts

by: Michelle Hirstius

Beignet

Fun fact...
Beignet is French for "fried dough"

Carousel

Fun fact...
the City Park Carousel built in 1906 is one of only a few wood carved carousels in the country!

French Bread

Fun fact... during the French Revolution, French Bread became the "Bread of Equality" by a Napoleonic decree.

Jazz

Fun fact... Jazz has been around since 1910. One of the most famous Jazz musicians is New Orleans own Louis Armstrong!

Queen

Fun fact...
the Mardi Gras Queen started around 1870 and she was picked by being the lucky lady with a golden bean inside her king cake.

Taffy

Fun fact...
   Taffy was originally made for cleaning your teeth, but then flavors were added and now we enjoy Taffy as a sweet treat!

Want more Juju?!
Collect ALL of her adventures :)

Down in da bayou we find a voodoo doll named Juju.
Juju is no ordinary voodoo doll;
she happens to be the one Marie has been looking for. Juju comes alive with a "good deeds" spell in the pages of this delightful fable where we find just the beginning of many adventures. Juju was created to show the positive things in life.

This year Santa gets in a pickle and stuck in da bayou. Thank goodness Juju is there to help. She uses her "good deeds" spell on some gators and they start to fly, that way they can finish delivering all the presents! Find out the beginning of where the Cajun Claus comes from.

Juju has a trick to learning numbers 1 through 20! She puts a cajun twist to an old classic nursery rhyme we all know. 1...2... start your roux! That is just the beginning, there are also plenty of counting exercises too. 10% of proceeds from this book is donated to WYES a Public Broadcasting Station in New Orleans, LA.

Easter is at a halt! Find out how Juju saves Easter and learn about a magical land full of color and candy... Ever wonder where all the delicious Easter candy, Elmer Heavenly Hash, Golden Brick and Pecan eggs come from, now you will. .. .

Juju thinks it's an ordinary day to go for a ride in her airboat when she sees a crowd gathered. She finds out that a puppy is stuck in a pile of fallen trees, Juju uses her "good deeds" spell and shrinks. She rescues the puppy and brings him to a shelter so they can fix his paw and later Juju decides to adopt him. Juju teaches children how they can do "good deeds" at their local animal shelter and care for their pets. 10% of proceeds go to the Humane Society of Louisiana.

Follow Juju on facebook, instagram, twitter, Pinterest and YouTube
www.JujuTheGoodVoodoo.com

Comprehension Questions:

1. We learned Beignet is a French word. What does it mean?

2. What words stood for the letters: D, G and M?

3. Why do we cook Red Beans and Rice on Mondays?

4. What is Louisiana's state bird? and where else can it be found for Louisiana?

5. What's another name for the French Quarter?

* answers on next page*

Follow Juju on facebook, instagram, twitter, Pinterest and YouTube
www.JujuTheGoodVoodoo.com

Answers:

1. Fried dough

2. Dragonfly, Gumbo and Magnolia

3. It's known as day for doing laundry.

4. Pelican and can be found on the Louisiana state flag, seal and bicentennial quarter.

5. Vieux Carré

Follow Juju on facebook, instagram, twitter, Pinterest and YouTube
www.JujuTheGoodVoodoo.com

CPSIA information can be obtained
at www.ICGtesting.com
Printed in the USA
BVOW10s0857270916

463416BV00001B/4/P